BODIE: Ghost Town

BODIE: Ghost Town

Thomas W. Moore

South Brunswick and New York: A. S. Barnes and Company
London: Thomas Yoseloff Ltd

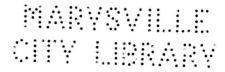

© 1969 by A. S. Barnes and Co., Inc.

Library of Congress Catalogue Card Number: 68–27229

A. S. Barnes and Co., Inc.

Cranbury, New Jersey 08512

Thomas Yoseloff Ltd

18 Charing Cross Road

London, W.C. 2, England

6863

Printed in the United States of America

Dedicated to the members of the Ancient and Honorable Order of E Clampus Vitus who gave unstintingly of their time and energies to make possible the preservation of Bodie as a monument to our pioneer heritage; and with acknowledgment to Kay Stokes who typed, and typed, and typed.

BODIE

"Goodbye, God, I'm going to Bodie." This prayer burst from the lips of a little girl in Truckee City the night she learned the family would be moving to the bad and bawdy mining town.

Bodie

San Francisco

Los Angeles

GOLDEN CALIFORNIA, 1850

BODIE: Ghost Town

THE COURT HOUSE, BRIDGEPORT, CALIFORNIA

This is the county seat of Mono County. Originally, the county seat was in Aurora which a later survey party found to be actually located in Nevada! Bodie records and mining claims were filed here. The cannon in the foreground was cast by the Bodie Iron Works. The town of Bodie is 22 miles SE from here and off Highway 395.

11

BODIE STATE HISTORIC PARK PLAQUE

William Bodey perished in a blizzard during the winter of 1859–60. In the following summer, the first lode claim was made. The oldest building, known as the Hydro Building, was built in 1861, and the first of many mining corporations was formed in 1863. Bodie gained national recognition as the "Wildest Town in the West." Fires and the elements reduced these buildings to what they are today. Bodie was made a State Park in 1962.

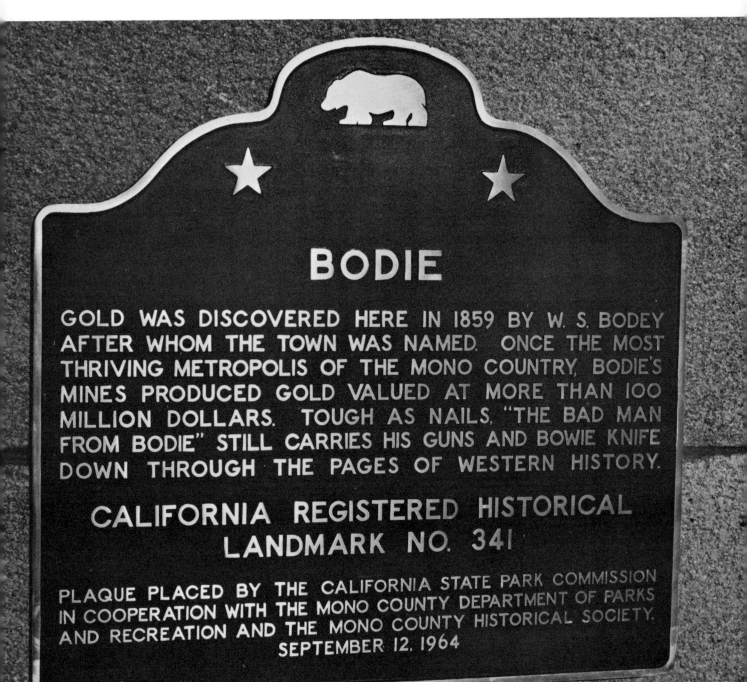

BODIE

GOLD WAS DISCOVERED HERE IN 1859 BY W. S. BODEY AFTER WHOM THE TOWN WAS NAMED. ONCE THE MOST THRIVING METROPOLIS OF THE MONO COUNTRY, BODIE'S MINES PRODUCED GOLD VALUED AT MORE THAN 100 MILLION DOLLARS. TOUGH AS NAILS, "THE BAD MAN FROM BODIE" STILL CARRIES HIS GUNS AND BOWIE KNIFE DOWN THROUGH THE PAGES OF WESTERN HISTORY.

CALIFORNIA REGISTERED HISTORICAL LANDMARK NO. 341

PLAQUE PLACED BY THE CALIFORNIA STATE PARK COMMISSION IN COOPERATION WITH THE MONO COUNTY DEPARTMENT OF PARKS AND RECREATION AND THE MONO COUNTY HISTORICAL SOCIETY. SEPTEMBER 12, 1964

13

BODIE BLUFF, THE TOWN AND STANDARD MILL

This is the view seen from Boot Hill, the cemetery of the infamous. Tourists are all gone now and I am alone. Alone?? I hear the whisper of the wind in the tall grass. The shadows lengthen as the dying sun dips behind the cemetery hill. There is a sudden chill in the air, and I find myself listening for pianos tinkling in the saloons, the boisterous shouts of the miners, and the squeals of the painted ladies. In 1878–1881 hardly a day passed when the druggist didn't find a dead man on his door step—"a man for breakfast" the town called it. During these years over 10,000 people lived in the town. In 1890 there were only 2,000 souls and it was all over for Bodie. These are the only ones who stayed behind.

14

15

HOMES OF THE RESPECTED
CITIZENRY, BODIE

These flimsy wooden dwellings withstood temperatures of minus forty degrees and snows twenty feet deep. Winds up to seventy miles per hour were recorded. One of the houses belongs to Annie Donnelly, leader of the social elite of the town. Her running social battle with Lottie Johl, from the red light district, provided the town with much conversational material for the long severe winters.

PARK AVENUE HOMES

Like Park Avenues of other cities, these were the homes of the elite, the solid citizens whose family predecessors lie buried in the respectable cemetery of Bodie. It is certain that this is the loftiest Park Avenue in the world at 8400 feet. Fraternal organizations like the Masons, Odd Fellows, the Miner's Union, Rebekahs, Knights of Pythias, Knights Templar provided the social activity, with each order having its "Grand Ball" on a different national holiday. These affairs were very elaborate. The ladies dressed in evening dresses with long kid gloves and fans. The men also rose to these occasions by wearing black suits and string ties. For both men and women, it was a badge of distinction to be considered a good dancer. At midnight a grand supper was served at one of the hotels.

THE UNITED STATES LAND OFFICE

Mine organizations such as the McClinton, the Red Cloud, the Bulwer and the Blackhawk all had their legal beginnings here. The leadership of big men like George S. Dodge, F. M. Bechtel, William Irwin, H. M. Yerington and Leland Stanford led to syndicated mining interests. There were scrambles among individual prospectors too, for the ore produced a very rich yield. In 1879, stock in the Bodie Mining company rose from 50 cents to $54 a share.

A THROUGH-THE-WINDOW DETAIL

Paraphernalia of existence, as seen through a store window, is significant in its range of variety. A pan to cook with, snowshoes to travel with, a shovel to dig with, and a bed pan—all bespeak of fried suppers, deep snows, buried ore and sickness. It was a hard life. The embossed sheet-metal wall covering was much used in the district. Wood in all forms was scarce, for Bodie lies above the timberline.

MAIN STREET ARCHITECTURE

These are original buildings surviving three fires and standing since 1878. The Miners' Union Hall with the wooden sidewalk was the focal point for the district organization meetings. The hall was also the social center of the town. It was here that Lottie Johl, a butcher's wife, formerly of "Maiden Lane," was unmasked at a high society masquerade ball. Up to that moment, she had been the judge's selection for the most beautiful "lady." She left with head held high but there were tears in her eyes. Years later, during an illness, she was given a deadly drug by mistake instead of proper medicine and died in the night.

DRUG STORE WINDOW DETAIL

The druggist often became the gunshot doctor and dead men were usually deposited on his front doorstep each morning. "Gold is where you find it" and news of a new strike close by would sometimes empty the town overnight. During these times, a meal would be completely abandoned. Before vandals came, table settings were to be found, as if the inhabitants had heard the news at dinner and left immediately.

24

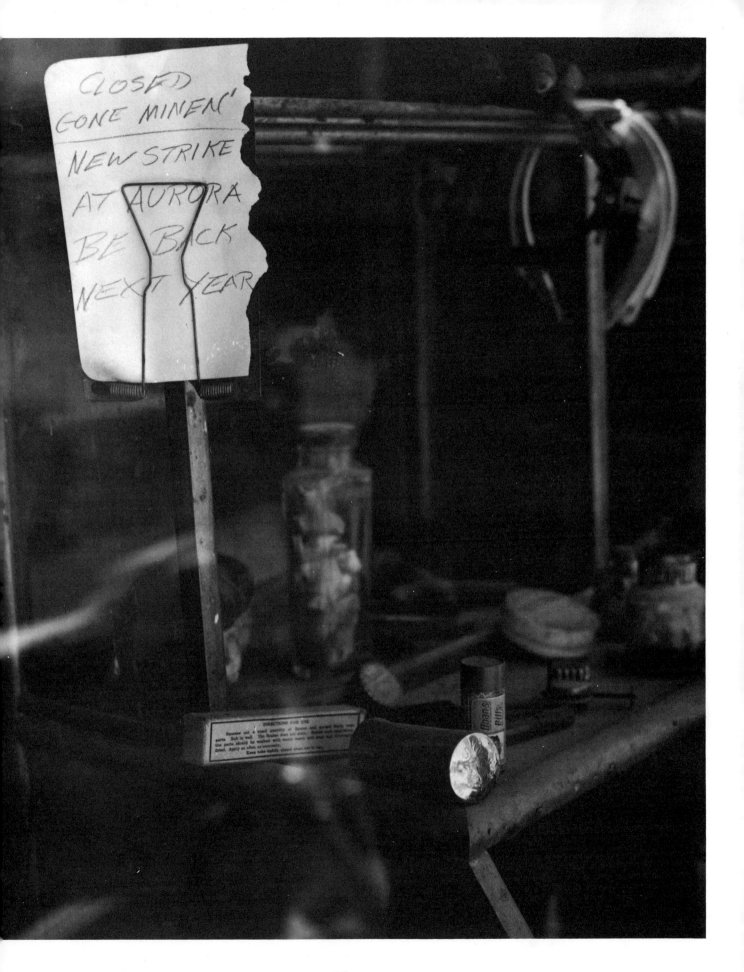

BOONE'S BRICK STORE

Later a café, this building was originally Harvey Boone's store. He also owned the stable and livery business. In 1878 it was mostly a wooden town of 250 structures with about 100 additional habitations and shelters around the mines. The town was decimated by disastrous fires in 1892, 1932 and 1946. Main Street was a mile long in 1879, solidly lined with one and two story frame buildings. Every other business establishment was a saloon and gambling hall.

WINDOW AND WALL DETAIL

Within these buildings life pulsed and died. These old boards witnessed fame and fortune— and misfortune. They housed the famous like Theodore Hoover, brother of our former president, and Tom Leggett, first to transmit electrical power by wires for a considerable distance. There was H. M. Yerington, the railroad builder of Nevada, and later governor; Harry Gorham, who owned the Santa Monica tract; and Florence Molinelli, world famous on the legitimate stage. Yes, and the infamous lived here too. Those girls from Virgin Alley and Maiden Lane like Rosa May, Emma Goldsmith, and "Madame Mustache." There was "Bad Mike" and "Pioche Kelly, who shot Charlie Jardine; and James de Roche, strung up by the 601 Vigilante Committee. These are all buried on Boot Hill. There was little Pretty Maggie, Indian girl who became the mistress of Tong Sing Wo. Later, she became an opium addict and was abandoned the night the Chinese all left town. In her agony she committed suicide by eating poisoned parsnip roots. Leland Stanford missed a fortune by selling his mine interest too soon. In time it produced 4 million dollars in gold!

A LEANING SALOON

There were seven breweries in operation at one time in Bodie. In 1929, the town was raided by prohibition officers. The bootleg whiskey was so good the officers took plenty of evidence back with them. The saloons were fined heavily, but as soon as the officers were out of sight, the bars were running wide open. It's been said that miners just can't work on soda pop.

LOW-BED CARGO WAGON

This wagon probably hauled more beer and whiskey than anything else. Bodie beer was most excellent because of the water. Besides the gold, it was Bodie's greatest export. Whiskey was shipped into town a hundred barrels at a time. The wagon drivers took their drinks enroute. They would hammer up the iron hoop, drive a nail through the stave and then pull the nail out. From the little stream that gushed forth, the drivers would drink their fill. The hole was then plugged up with a wood sliver and the hoop was hammered back down into place. Whiskey sold at two drinks for a quarter, or ten cents for a single drink. You were in disgrace if you bought a single drink with your "short bit."

MAIN STREET BY MORNING LIGHT

Bodie knew how to celebrate! Early on Fourth
of July mornings the children were routed out of
bed by a great dynamite blast set off on the top
of Bodie Bluff. The mines were shut down and
by ten o'clock the citizens were aligned on both
sides of the street to watch the "Grand Parade."
All the lodge members marched in full dress.
Bands, drum corps, Veterans of the Mexican and
Civil Wars, firemen's hook and ladder companies
all marched, too. There was bunting on all the
store fronts and flags everywhere. For this day,
and even on the day of William Bodey's funeral,
large wagon loads of green foliaged trees were
cut in Cottonwood Canyon, hauled up to Bodie
and placed in holes dug side by side. When morning dawned, there was a solid wall of greenery
along both sides of Main Street for the entire
length of it! For Bodie, where no flower or tree
ever grew, this was the summit of embellish-
ment.

GREEN STREET BY GOLDEN LIGHT

Where Green and Main Streets intersect, it was great sport to have a badger fight. Badgers brought into town by Indians were eagerly bought by "sporting" men. Badger dogs were rounded up and bets were placed. Usually the contest was between one dog and one badger. Sometimes when the badger whipped every dog matched, the whole pack was turned loose on him. Not far from where this picture was taken, to the right over by the Standard Mill, the first killing took place. Union Pacific Jack and his buddy argued over who was the meaner. Citizens called it a good draw and thankfully buried both of them! The last killing occurred when "Red" Roe, mean, educated, quoting Shakespeare and the Scriptures, a bully and a prankster, jokingly challenged little "Dutchy" to wrestle. Dutchy, frightened, thinking Red meant to kill him, borrowed a shotgun and emptied both barrels. Thus passed Bodie's last bad man, a victim of his own reputation.

THE BODIE JAIL

Inner cells barely large enough for one man are fronted by an outer office with these windows. The really dangerous prisoners were strung up or run out of town by the "601 Vigilante Committee." Surviving prisoners were kept in the jail at Bridgeport. This was a holding jail used mostly for drunks. It is an original building. "Two Gun" Al was the most frequent habitué. Once after a fight he was jailed, but pals would bring him whiskey—pouring it into his cup which he would hold through the bars. Once he was jailed for tying his horse to a prostitute's piano leg, and once for riding his horse into Ernest Mark's saloon. Al died in bed and was buried on Boot Hill that same afternoon.

A TYPICAL BLACKSMITH SHOP

Such a shop provided the wagon crane that the "601" Committee used to lynch Joseph DeRoche. They hung him over the very stains that marked the place where DeRoche shot unarmed Johnny Treloar in cold blood. DeRoche had been paying unwanted attentions to Treloar's wife. At a dance on the night of January 14th, 1881, the matter finally erupted into the one-sided argument and Treloar lay dead in the snow.

36

THE VAULT OF THE BODIE BANK

Having escaped two disastrous fires, it would have been too miraculous to have escaped a third. This was Jim Cain's bank. He never lost faith in Bodie, buying out his partners each time they wanted to invest in greener fields elsewhere. The bank was robbed of $4,000 in 1914. The thieves were really seeking a $10,000 gold bar which had been shipped out the day before. While it was suspected who the robbers were, the case was never pursued. There were well-known family connections. Besides, mining people were rather tolerant of gold seekers—even this type of "high grading."

38

GREEN STREET LOOKING WEST

The large building in the center was the school house. Originally, it was the Bon Ton Lodging House until pressed into service after some reluctant students burned the school house down in 1879. The original school house was located farther up the hill. A schoolmaster named Cook had his beard pulled in hand-to-hand combat with some of the older students. One schoolmaster named McCarty used a long black poker to keep order and whip that school into shape.

THE STANDARD COMPANY

The first and largest of the big mining companies, it was first called the Bunker Hill Mine. The Company passed through various hands until 1863 when it was consolidated into a new company headed by Leland Stanford, then Governor of California. The Governor paid a visit to the camp, unknowingly stood within a few feet of millions in gold, and declared he wouldn't give $500 for the whole district! Six years after he withdrew, "his" mine had made millions. Mules were used to haul the ore cars at the various levels. A half grown white mule named Jerry was lowered to the 500 foot level, never again to see the light of day. When there was a fire in the mine, he suffocated because he had grown too big to be lifted out. He was buried in the mine shaft.

BROKEN WINDOW DETAIL

Like an empty eye socket set darkly in a lifeless skull, this window looks out over a lifeless town. The little fragment of glass, like a frozen tear, lingers in the corner of this wooden eye that once saw some happiness, mostly despair, but all of life lived fully. Inside there is only torn wallpaper, dusty broken furniture, a rusty bed spring and loose boards in a floor covered with dust and bird droppings. The town is truly dead.

WILLIAM S. BODEY GRAVE MARKER

William S. Bodey, for whom the town is named, prospected here, discovered gold here and died here. He was caught in a blizzard returning home from Monoville in November of 1859. The following spring, Black Taylor, his partner, found the bones and bowie knife and buried them on the spot. In the boom year of 1879, the bones were exhumed and then buried somewhere up on the hill. This obelisk was sculpted in 1880 for Bodey's grave. When President Garfield was assassinated, the town, caught up in a burst of patriotism, agreed to place this monument with an inscription to the President's memory in the Masonic Cemetery. Only sagebrush covers the grave where Bodey is actually buried.

47

AN ANGEL IN BODIE?

Yes, but not voluntarily. This one, frozen in stone, marking the grave of a child in the respectable cemetery above Boot Hill, points up so typically the fate of the young and less hearty. Death from pneumonia caused by inadequate housing for the severe winters of minus forty degree temperatures further decimated the population.

THE ROAD BACK HOME

Over the church steeple can be seen a car-raised cloud of dust on the road back to the cities. Cities that were built by some of Bodie's gold if not by some of her men. Mining Company President, Leland Stanford, was Governor of the State; Superintendent William Irwin built the Irwin Hotel in San Francisco; electrician Paul Milton Dowing was a chief executive of the Pacific Gas and Electric Company; Harry Gorham owned the land of Santa Monica. Strong men these, along with others mentioned in this book, but gamblers and saloon men claim it was the first lynching and the first church that killed Bodie. "A hangin' and a church will kill any camp." Bad men do not bring good times to a town, but they seem to take them with them when they go.

BOONE'S STORE AND BODIE CAFE

Open to the elements of wind, rain and snow, you earned a full cup walking to the café for that morning coffee. It was here, after the mines played out and 20,000 souls had left, that a man could hear the latest news, get a lead on a job, smoke, joke with the fellows and gather himself for the day. The spirit of camaraderie was real, born of common need and lack, no longer from a common bottle.

THE METHODIST CHURCH

One of two churches for the whole Bodie community, it was built in 1879 and presided over by Reverend Hinkle. The Catholic Church was founded by Father John Cassin in about the same year. It was located on the opposite side of town and called St. John's—after himself. The Bishop had told the Father to name it after the man who contributed the most towards its construction. The Catholic Church was burned to the ground in 1928 but the original cross is on exhibit in the Bodie Museum. The Methodist Church was restored in 1928 by E. J. Clinton of the Clinton Cafeteria in San Francisco, himself a miner in Bodie during the 1920's. Even here, there were a few who said, "Lord, I have loved the habitation of Thy house, and the place where Thine honour dwelleth. Gather not my soul with sinners, nor my life with bloody men." Psalm 26:8, 9.

THE HEILSHORN MORGUE AND BODIE BLUFF

"Shotgun" Johnnie Heilshorn, thief, dope fiend, rounder, grave robber, undertaker and dealer in second hand coffins, used the brick building in the center for his morgue. He was found dead in a Chinatown opium bunk, presumably from an overdose of morphine. One can still see the hills pimpled with diggins'—the acne scars of abandoned claims. It is estimated by mining engineers that there is still a $150 million in gold here, but it can't be mined profitably at $35 per ounce.

52

MAIN STREET AT EVENING

A lonesome street now with only grazing cows to "people" it, this was really the best time of the day for Bodie's main roadway. The street was once lined with wooden sidewalks and benches in front of every store and saloon. The men, a good supper inside them, a good cigar to relax them, and a few drinks to expand them, would toss hard money down for the kids to "peg the coin." This was done quite accurately with their string tops. The first boy to hit the coin with his top kept the coin. Sometimes these coins were gold pieces! Later, when darkness was complete, the street would echo the sounds of boisterous merriment or tragedy.

THE HOME OF J. S. CAIN, INDUSTRIALIST

James Stewart Cain, a businessman with the golden touch, used his brain and his money to really establish Bodie. He set up a lumber mill, barge and railroad system to bring wood and timbers for home and mine construction. He leased ground from the Standard Mine and took out $90,000 in 90 days! He bought the Bodie Bank and, as a large stockholder in the Standard, he was instrumental in pioneering the history making Green Creek hydroelectric plant. At great personal expense he established two additional plants at Lee Vining and Rush Creek in Mono County. He and E. J. McCone of Virginia City bought all the old mine tailings around Bodie. Using the new cyanide process, they gleaned a fortune from the discarded diggings. Cain eventually took over the Standard when his Midnight Mine was "highgraded" by the Standard. The ensuing litigation damages were so high the compromise gave him the control.

WAGON WHEEL HUB STUDY

Furrowed by time, this wheel, still strong and sturdy, is a tribute to the wheelwright. Groaning under its loads as wagon wheels do, perhaps it turned over the lofty torturous Sierra mountain roads of Tioga and Sonora summit passes to bring Bodie's gold to the Vanity Fair cities of the world below.

58

RED LIGHT DISTRICT AND CHINATOWN AREA

North of town, outside the weal so to speak, was the Bodie Chinatown, the central street of which was at right angles to Main Street. It was very narrow and crowded with little wooden shacks. The two and three story buildings in this area were the "Mercantile Establishments" with stores below and luxurious dens upstairs. The dens of Chinatown were significant contributors to the killings in Bodie. In most dens the opium bunks were on the street floor. One could look into these places and see men, and women too, lying there smoking opium while others sat around a table playing fan-tan. Still farther to the north, in the area of that first building, was the red light district. "Maiden Lane" and "Virgin Alley" were the main streets of it. Rosa May of "The Highgrade" was queen of the town. Emma Goldsmith of "The Ozark," "The May Time," "Beautiful Doll," and "Madame Moustache" are just a few of the most famous people and "places" of the district. The "Madame" was so named because of her aversion to men with hair on their faces. Rosa May, an angel of mercy during a pneumonia epidemic, died of the disease herself and was buried in the out-cast cemetery, Boot Hill.

AGED WINDOW DETAIL

Panes coated with the dust of time—how long did you stare westward, Window, before no one cared to look? This window in a sagging house high up the Green Street Hill still retains much glass. Now it, too, shows signs of natural and tourist attrition. Each year more lenses are stripped from the eye sockets of these old houses.

A BODIE "STILL-LIFE" OF TODAY

This pictorial study shows all of the elements of present-day Bodie. In the foreground are tin cans, basins, broken bottles, bricks and bedsprings everywhere; the wooden wheels are lifting belt pulley sheaves from the mines. Beyond these are the rusting parts of an automobile against a background of treeless hills. Waiting on the hillside is a forsaken home sheeted with tin from flattened three-gallon cans, and beyond that the open yawning mine entrance.

64

BODIE'S BACKYARDS AND TRACKS

Wood was scarce and with winter temperatures 40° below zero a backyard wood pile was like gold. Tracks would tell if anyone was thieving, but tracking and catching were different things. A hole was drilled in a log and black powder inserted and plugged. When that stick was stolen, the trap was sprung. The next cold winter evening the town was startled by a shack explosion up on the hill. It was Bodie's Buffalo Bill, blown out of his house, stolen goods lying all around him, his red face covered by grimy black soot.

ORE CARTS ON GREEN STREET

Loading these carts by pick and shovel digging in the narrow confines of a slanting mine tunnel was hard backbreaking work. In 1881, when the gold rush excitement had begun to subside, there were 500 miners working in company mines. The wages were $4.00 a day for miners to $6.00 a day for foremen. Whole families lived quite comfortably on these wages.

66

67

THE HOUSE ON THE HILL

Warm summer days have all slipped by. October Sun, where have you gone? Have you, too, abandoned Bodie? The wind whistles through these threadbare buildings moving curtain tatters in some swaying ethereal cadence. The lowering sky portends the winter's snows. The late fall day, grey and gloomy, is cold and blustery. The wooden structure to the left of the house is a toilet tunnel. There is also one to the rear of the house against which firewood was stacked. The tunnels provided access to these facilities during the heaviest snows. Imagine walking through that dark tunnel late at night by flickering candlelight with the screeching wind searching for every crack and wall opening to snuff out your candle. Could I have done it at seven, ten or fifteen years?

68

ABANDONED CHAIR BY THE WINDOW

Empty chair, empty room, empty house, empty town—perhaps. But there *is* a sense of presence here. You feel it everywhere. You feel it as you look into these old houses and walk these old streets. It is as if the person has just stepped into the next room. Did they? And then time stood still.

70

POWER AND TELEPHONE POLE
OF BODIE

The electrification of the world as we know it today began at Bodie in 1892. While electrical power had been developed it was only used at its source of development. Tom Legett, Superintendent of the Stanford Mine, was convinced that electricity would run the hoists and mills cheaper than steam. The hydroelectric plant at Green Creek was built along with a thirteen-mile power transmission line to Bodie. The mines used most of the electricity of course, but some of the affluent homes were electrified.

72

WINDSWEPT CEMETERY

Contrasting ludicrously in brilliant color against the driven snow, waxen flowers of summer care startle the midwinter visitor by their apparent freshness.

MYSTERIOUS MONO LAKE BASIN

The great eastern slope of the Sierra Nevada Mountains forms an impenetrable barrier to California and the cities of San Francisco and Los Angeles. This is Paiute Indian country and the briney desert area of Mono Lake. Salt! Great white pillars of salt are thrust up out of the water like satanic sculpted monoliths. Lumber for Bodie was barged across the lake from saw mills on the south shore. At the north coast it was loaded on to flat cars and railroaded into Bodie. These were just two of J. S. Cain's many enterprises. In the distance clinging to the steep slope of the mountains is the city of Lee Vining, closest "civilization" to Bodie. The haunting sense of presence begins here.

SHOOTERS TOWN AT HIGH NOON

Ghostly, like some lost moon city, remote, cold, foreboding, Bodie lies beyond the shelter of forest or hill accepting the onslaughts of winter—stoic—but slowly eroding. When spring finally comes to these mountains, there will be less of her to fire the imagination of the dreamer and his offspring's piping voice will be heard to say distainfully, "Is this all?"

MAIN STREET DRIFT

Weather-stained buildings stark against the drifted snow, this scene was oft repeated on wintry mornings. The inhabitants were immobilized by such storms. With no one moving about, this scene is exactly as it was on a January morning in 1932, or 1920 or 1892. The town is directly beneath the course of the major airlines to the East. Silver jet trails saber the sky, and standing here snowbound and isolated I am humbled by the contrast that time has wrought.

ABANDONED CHAISE CARRIAGE

Like a racer that stumbled and fell, never to arise, frozen where he lay, this carriage must have flown over the grassy Bodie plain in summer behind a high spirited filly. No ordinary carriage this, it was designed for speed and elegance and fortunate was the young man who could wheedle it from his father to go a-courtin'.

ABANDONED CAR BODY

A world apart in point of concept yet over-parked similarly as the carriage at the intersection of the street of abandonment and the boulevard of broken dreams. This flivver body, doors akimbo, black against the snow, shows that Bodie kept pace with the rest of the world in the pursuit of culture and progress. A car was a car was a car in Bodie as well as anywhere else.

SAGE BRUSH AND CORN SNOW

A contrast of textures and patterns, like Bodie itself, tender and callous, showing light and shadow, good and evil, achievement and dissipation, alone in a field of white, alone here at the top of the world, isolated by the camera lens.

THE GRAVE OF LOTTIE JOHL

Courted, wooed and wedded out of the red light district by successful butcherman Eli Johl, Lottie was shunned by Bodie society. She was denied her first prize when unmasked at a ball Eli insisted she attend. Lottie was a true and good wife to Eli but the town rule was inflexible. When she died because of a careless druggist, she was allowed the farthest corner of the "respectable" cemetery. Eli put up this fence and every Memorial Day decorated the grave with canopy, picture and bunting. People came to laugh at Eli's "Carnival Booth" and left with tears after seeing his love and grief.

BOONE'S STORE AND BODIE CAFE

Open to the elements of wind, rain and snow,
you earned a full cup walking to the café for that
morning coffee. It was here, after the mines
played out and 20,000 souls had left, that a man
could hear the latest news, get a lead on a job,
smoke, joke with the fellows and gather himself
for the day. The spirit of camaraderie was real,
born of common need and lack, no longer from a
common bottle.

88

THE BODIE FIREHOUSE WITH BELL

Organized since the boom days of 1878, the Bodie Volunteer Fire Department was always a well-drilled and efficient organization. Engine and hose cart units were separate and competed with one another. The hook and ladder cart carried a hundred rubber buckets hanging from its frame. Officers wore red rubberized hats and belts with emblazed emblems to show the rank of the wearer. The department was quite a spectacle in the July Fourth parades. The Fireman's Ball in winter was the gala social event of the year. This bell sounded the alarm for many fires including the disastrous 1892 and 1932 fires. Each time the bell was salvaged from the ashes of the burned firehouse.

THE BODIE SCHOOL

This was the Bon Ton Lodging House in 1881 when Joseph DeRoche was imprisoned to prevent his being lynched after the Treloar murder. He did escape from here, was caught by the "601" and lynched—hanged where Treloar's blood stained the snow. The building has been standing since 1879 and became the school after the original school was burned by a student.

93

SNOW-BOUND GRAVE MARKER

Buried, buried. Rest in peace James Gordon beneath your downy blanket of snow. No tourist walks this cemetery today. All is still and waiting. Do friendly ghosts freeze? Hibernate? Whereas in summer I sensed an ethereal sharing of Bodie's past, here in winter I sense open hostility. In summer I was allowed to partake— vicariously. In winter my presence is resented. The sudden wind, the cold, the threatening clouds all tell me to leave now.

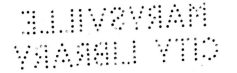